Shad

a poetry collection

Stefanie Briar

Stefanie Briar

ISBN: 9798788859804

Instagram: @stefanie.briar.poetry

TikTok: @stefaniebriarpoetry

Release Date: 1/11/2022

Kindle Direct Publishing

Cover design by Mitch Green

Instagram: @mitch_grn

"Don't go, you're half of me now,
but I'm hardly stood proud.
I said it, almost.

Oh, I've been low, but dammit,
I bet it didn't show.
It was heaven a moment ago,
I had it, almost.
We had it, almost.

I can't seem to let myself leave you,
but I can't breathe anymore.
I can't seem to not need you,
and I can't breathe anymore."

-Novo Amor
"Repeat Until Death"

For those who love with all they have.

This book contains some content and language
intended for mature audiences.

Note: the ➔ symbol denotes a poem that
continues on to the next page.

I love like an inferno;
it spreads and grows
until everything else
you've ever known
ceases to exist.

So if it's me you want to love,
I hope you're ready to *burn*.

Shades of Ruin

I burn like a wildfire
that reaches the city—
less measurable headway,
more obvious casualties.

I take out the high-rise
and the mountain,
collapse the steel,
melt the snow.

When I run out of destruction,
I'd bet the forest floor
that I'll have carved a path
right up to your door.

All this to say,
I hope you'd open the door
and welcome the flames.

4

Love me in all my shadowed places,
the dark spaces I tiptoe around,
the ones I dare not make eye contact with
for fear of what may be seen.

Touch and kiss them tenderly,
until my darkness gives way to morning.

I was born for the kind of love that hurts.

Once my love touches you,
it burrows its hooks inside
the hollows in your chest
where no light has ever landed.
Long after we abandon ship,
you'll still hold me close within
because no one has ever
loved you like this,
leveling your walls with a fingertip.

I'm a wild kind of fearless
the depths of which
you will never know
or let go of again.

I am the fire that never dies.

You will roam this earth
for the rest of your days
cursed to find me in everyone
and everything.

I am someone you lose your life to
without ever noticing.
I think it's because
I love *without mercy*.

Oh, look at you...
I am churning with an ache
that hollows my stomach
and swallows the acid.
I'm studying you
like my life depends on it,
like you're the first test
I might not ace.
I am woefully underprepared,
staring at the veins in your hands
and wishing to swim them
like the thin channels of dirt
underneath your nails.

Your hair falls across your face
just the right way,
and I am as undone
as the buttons you'll soon fumble with.
I write your name on my ribcage
in the sincerity of my blood,
and I swear I will adore you
until the sun combusts
and the moon dies
and the mountains crumble
and the ocean dries
like the skin chapped across your lip
that I want to bite.

You're nervous,
so am I.
You're right across the table,
and I want to flip it across the room
and fly into your arms.

We will fall like stars,
golden into a horizon we can't yet see.

We are about to be *everything.*
We will cross every line,
jump into uncharted seas,
and pray for just the right amount of
drowning.

I don't know how to be ready,
but one look in your eyes,
and I would follow you anywhere.

It's as though I handed you a key,
and you unlocked everything inside of me
that I kept hidden or held at bay.

There went my madness,
my defenses,
my pretense,
and my doubt.

There was just
you,
you,
you,
no turning back now.

You touched me back to life,
kissed me unglued,
shook me loose,
inhabited my head like a bad habit.

A gentle click,
a soft entry,
and you had me

melting

a w a y.

I fold into you
like the page corners
of my favorite novels.
We *sigh* verses of poetry
into the bindings
of a morning
                   well
                        spent.

Shades of Ruin

There are prisms on your body
dancing in the light of morning,
drifting through the gossamer
of softly swaying curtains.

Later on,
in the fleeting glow of golden hour,
tiny rainbows will flower softly
upon the warm canvas of your skin.

Light finds you as I once did,
an accident that is no accident.

There's no explaining this:
how after a mere glance,
the brush of hands,
and a single kiss,
we are absolutely convinced
that we have done this before...

many times,
many lives,
untold stories our love has lived
reflected back in our eyes,
waiting for rediscovery.

There are worlds in you,
and I must have loved you
in
     e v e r y
          one.

If we are what we love,
then I am whatever *you* are made of.

I think I was somehow
homesick for you
long before we'd meet.

I lived knowing
that my "home" had a
h e a r t b e a t.

Shades of Ruin

Love me
until oblivion
paints your portrait
behind my eyelids,
sinking by eons
into the distance
that *never separates us.*

How can be it be
that such softness can coexist
with an all-consuming need
to ruin you for all of eternity?

We are the flowers and the fire.
I am the rose that blooms in flames;
you are honey wafting from the smoke.

We are everything that makes no sense,
and *everything that does.*

It seems
that all your demons
are shaped like my silhouette,
casting shadows on the walls,
caught in spotlights overhead.

You take them by the hand,
and ask them to dance.

You,
with the nimble fingers
that render my mouth loud
and my mind mute...

Come on over tonight.
I've got nothing to do
but *y o u.*

Shades of Ruin

"You will be the ruin of me",
you hissed into my ear,
fingers tearing into cotton and sin.
How I laughed then...
as if I held your life in my hands,
as you put yours in all the places
you hadn't yet seen,
and would never be able to forget.

You gave me a standing ovation,
and I took it in my hands,
moving you to where the honey meets the hive.
We brought each other back to life:
you gave me the hunger on your breath,
the salt in your kiss,
the gold on your tongue.
We were pulse and bare skin
until
          kingdom

                    c o m e.

No touching my soul
until you dirty my thoughts
with your fingerprints,
turn my damp earth,
uproot the eldest trees,
gore the underbelly,
flay the deepest worms.

You did.

You laid quick waste
to all I placed in your way,
so I stole back the ocean,
and I gave myself to you:
yielding like split skin,
ripening and blooming red
at your fingertips.

You peel my onion-
hidden blood, bluing flesh,
a mess of mended bone
stripped to the marrow.
You build hearth and home
of my chest cavity;
I'm no gracious host,
but you stay anyway.

The clock is stuck
at the chimes of midnight,
the beginning or the end
(you wonder which I am),
but you tremble out the hour
when I am upon you:
the disease and the cure,
the door to other worlds.

→

Shades of Ruin

You open it,
(of course you do);
I kill you in the foxhole
under the same sky
that swallowed us to riddle.
I string your body up,
play us in the drum circle,
hunger in my hands
and war crimes on the brain.

Self-destructing moths
to the ruinous flame,
tiny kamikazes
into streetlight eyes:
I eat your softest demons
and you drink me faster
than I can start
to whet your appetite.

I'd watch you
collapse to your knees
and offer me your throat
for all of eternity,
and I burst into blood bubbles
at the sound of your name
across my temples.

We met,

and we went mad.

We lost our heads,
and admired them
as they sat on pikes
adorning the bridge.

We are a sight to behold,
even in our ruin.

Sometimes, you'd look at my mouth,
and imagine my blunt tongue was serrated—
sharpened to land cleanly
in all your vulnerable places.

It always did;
you were both repulsed
and turned on by it.

I'd watch you think:
"I'd let her destroy me."

In many ways,
I've done just that.

Tame love is love wasted;
the best love flays you open.

There you were at dinner,
your innards on my table,
playing into my sleight of hand,
bracing for the scalpel.

When I tore into you,
and you began to bleed freely,
you pulled me toward the bedroom,
begging "Finish me."

I did.

I am undressed down to
the naked wanting of you
that trembles my hands
and slows the words in my throat.

The only way to burn.

My favorite way to choke.

Shades of Ruin

Parking lot,
pressed up against the car,
I put my hand inside your waistband.

In front of a church,
I take you to a heaven
the congregation has never seen.

Through my face, the devil grins.

You growl "Let's go",
and you grab my hand;
we can't break in fast enough.

You lead me past the old, oak door,
pull me up onto the vacant altar,
a willing lamb for slaughter.

Make meat of me, darling.
I'll count the bruises
like a rosary.

I kneel before you.

Before long,
I am leaving my body
and inhabiting every cross on the wall.

I am weightless,
and floating,
and full of us.

I receive our holy communion
on my waiting tongue,
and I am born again.

I hear applause in the distance,
and I think it's the gods
I don't believe in.

We loved in **shades of ruin:**
the screaming red of first collision,
the deep blue of missing you,
the grey of the question mark days,
the black void of the end,
and the goldenrod of the beginning.

We were a kaleidoscope of hope,
a pavement-oil rainbow,
a palette that mixed and blurred
into a muddy, earthy brown.

Shades of Ruin

You buried yourself
into my chest like a hatchet,
wrote your name in my blood,
made yourself at home.

I am still bleeding to this day,
my sternum struggling to contain

what remains of us.

We meant far too much
to have deserved an ending
this *unceremonious.*

These nights are too long,
the days drag on and on,
and this world has lost its color
without you as my center.

You were never my reason for breathing,
but you allowed me to breathe more freely,
safe inside your light.

I now understand why it's said
that heartbreak is its own death;
my entire life is now a funeral pyre.

This love was my baptism by fire,
and I've never liked the cold.

I shiver in the winter
that your *void* left in my soul.

Everything inside of me
was mesmerized by love;
I had your body memorized,
made you my favorite song for months.

I miss when you were
just a skipped heartbeat away.
Now all I've got is a playlist
that is titled with your name.

Stefanie Briar

When my mind goes somewhere
that it shouldn't go,
and I almost turn off the road
at your exit,
the highway whispers "no",
and gently drives me home
to where water meets sky.

Somewhere deep inside,
my heart closes the door
shaped like you.

Shades of Ruin

I am tired of love like a storm;
what I need is an anchor.

With you, I lost my fucking mind.

I lost every label this life
has pinned to my chest:
reliable, responsible, rational,
every source vetted.
You took my identity
and drive a battering ram through it,
so I drove myself to the edge
and dove off the cliff,
imagining a trampoline
while staring at jagged terrain.

Who was I again?
I managed to forget,
but I liked it,
I loved it,
I lived for it,
I got off on it,
(sometimes literally).
Every morning,
I jumped from the plane
and never lost the rush:
Constant falling,
Falling,
Falling,
no crash landing,
no getting up.

Everywhere else,
I'm the evolved bitch on her hippie shit:
namaste, not gonna stay
if you can't level up with this.
But here I am,
seducing the snake in the grass,
acting immune to the venom,
pretending we're a match.

I wear your fingerprints 'round my neck,
a noose to send me off.
You come at me with chains,
and I can't reach your bedposts fast enough.

What the hell is wrong with me?

➔

I'm make-a-fake-account-just-to-see-your-
face crazy,
look-up-your-exes-to-see-if-I'm-prettier
crazy,
midnight-drive-past-your-house crazy,
write-every-song-about-you crazy,
think-of-you-when-I-touch-myself crazy.

I'm the driver who careens into the bay
just to feel something again,
hopped up on love and loneliness,
all out of you and fucks to give.

My inner mechanisms
aren't steampunk shiny anymore,
I weep in metallic keenings
and you want "cries in cottagecore".
It's like bleeding out
without knowing of a wound,
you lose yourself inside a bottle,
and I lose myself in you.

You are my teeming inner-life,
the yellow in every bruise,
the habit that I hate to hide,
the war I have to lose.
Internally, I scream
to be consumed by you,
to be nailed to your wall,
hung on your cross at noon.

I need to be your victory feast,
but you've stopped eating meat.

NEED! Want is not enough!
Want is soft as kittens,
and I need to be flattened, eradicated,
annihilated, finished.

This maddening dichotomy
is sadly nothing new.
I've long since **lost my shit** over you.

I worshipped your skin,
tasted you to death,
skinned you with my fingertips,
wore you like a dress
draped over my curves just right.

Our nights were endless,
and yet somehow
always over too soon.
I lost sight of everything
that wasn't full of you.

We were rootless trees
in the eye of the storm,
the wind that would carry us away
from the center of ourselves,
and pour us into something new.

We were fused
in breath
in sex
in bone
in blood
in love
in ruin.

This love was always destined

to end in *total* annihilation.

I miss the delicious shivering
that traveled the highway of my body
as you would kiss my throat,
gradually
        i n c h i n g
                your
                      way
                          below.

Your lips knew me like a backroad;
your hands traversed me
without ever needing a map.

I miss being *known* like that.

I want to say I'm tired of feeling played,
you come back just a little,
but then you never stay.
I want to be tired of doubting,
and running, and hiding,
but the truth is I'm addicted

to letting you fuck me:
up, over, and every way
but the way I most crave it.

I don't know why we happened,
why we couldn't skip this lifetime,
but I hear the Universe laughing
every time I start to cry
trying to bury borrowed time:
pathetic as delusion gets,
and dirty in a grave.

I miss brave hands in my hair,
a late winter basement first kiss,
flowers and a question in the fridge,
goddamn, I miss everything...
thighs parting for your lips,
your fingertips on my neck,
my pulse in my ears,
hell, I even miss your tears.

Who are we if not playing with fire,
if not burning with desire,
and screaming one another's names
every other waking moment
in perfect silence?

I'm so painfully human,
and the truth is
I   just   miss   you.

Shades of Ruin

They call me a mad woman,
and I am a mad, mean, *dirty* thing
when you're not mine to have.

I hate it that you're with her:
I hate her hair,
I hate her name,
I hate her pearlescent skin
that never sees the sun.
I hate that she's the one,
and I'm just the vacation home.

Unforgivably,
you chose winter over summer,
but I still make sure your Airbnb is clean.

I ball the sheets up in my hands and bite them,
while you're behind me shouting my name
into the corners of four walls that do not
belong to us.

Your secret love,
your clandestine fuck,
skin a few shades closer to sin
than you're used to.

And every time you go back to her,
you take me with you.

We fucked
like time was suspended,
and the answers to life lay between my legs;
you were there enough
to learn every one of them.

I go to your head like a hangover,
and you let me slip from the corner
of your mind that I occupy.
You think back to every panting breath:
bathed in sweat like holy water
as you gave yourself over to my kiss.
The stain of me never leaves your lips,
no matter how often you try
to spot-treat me from your life...
I remain the catalyst
of your sleepless nights.

I am the blood and the burn,
the rot and the bone,
the venom and the antidote,
the face in every goddamn photo
hanging gilded from your organs.

You think of me when you're with her,
and the golden thread unravels,
the tower falls;
the walls you've so carefully rendered
become dust in the wind.
You can only ever keep me out for a moment,
because when you're alone, eyes closed,
or buried deep inside of her,
and you're riding, writhing, rising...
it's still me.

It's always me you're seeing,
it's my hair you're pulling,
it's my back you're blowing out,
it's my name screaming echoes
off the walls of your heart,
your throat seized closed by the hand of
destiny.

➔

Shades of Ruin

She's moaning,

you're zoning out,
and it's us there together now.

Do I look as good as you remember,
looking back at you from over my shoulder,
smug as the devil?
I miss you so fucking much
that it makes me mean,
makes me evil.

And it's not enough
that she never even comes close
and doesn't even know it,
or that her fate is to share you with me
without a say in the matter.

You erupt with a grunt,
and it's raining in my dreams.

My memory holds you
as your breathing shallows into steady.
You sink into the bed
like it's made of my skin,
the poorly-hidden existence
of your excruciating need.

You love me to war and to ruin
in your wildest dreams.
You can run, but never hide.

There is no escaping me.

You think of me
at the least opportune moments,
and curse my presence upon this earth
in the same time and space as you.

You do not want to share me with the world,
and yet you cannot keep me for yourself.
You've learned to live   s-p-l-i-t
at the seams.

You straddle her and I like we are state lines.
You carry your love for me on your shoulders,
and your love for her on your left finger.

I sit on your back like a boulder,
and she is your shelter from the cold...
no wonder I am too much for you to hold.

What becomes of the "extra" love?
How do you live with loving two at once?
How does she not see you're still hung up on
me?

I told you.
I *warned* you.
My memory would not leave   q u i e t l y.

You find me most often in the dark,
when you can feel her warmth
and turn her into me.

You lay there,
you listen to her breathing,
picturing the rise and fall of my ribcage.

You pull her in closer,
and kiss her gently as moth's wings,
so as not to disturb the fantasy.

You tell yourself it's harmless,
that you're only missing me,
but I doubt she'd agree.

I hope she's sleeping soundly.
I hope she doesn't know

that you never moved on.

Stefanie Briar

You told me I was "it" for you:

your last call, your *last train home.*

You claimed that, after me,
there could be no one else.
After you closed the door on us,
you soon went searching...
a new distraction,
a new love,
a new body to warm your sheets,
a void in need of filling.

Meanwhile,
my heavy heart kept pounding,
erratic with the flailing daggers
of our dead-skin memory
landing lonely in my back.
My bed stayed cold and empty,
and I grieved so intensely
that I wondered if my soul
could escape through my eyes.

The last time we spoke, you told me,
"I'm trying, but I can't find anything
remotely close."

You should have known.

The paradox of tears:
they help you see *more* clearly,
and I can't say I like the truth.

Forget the promise of an afterlife,
I just need an after*you.*

You never got the best of me;
there wasn't time for that, and yet
I opened before you like a rose,
legs blooming apart, petals exposed,
flowing into groundwater.

I wanted you to poison my well,
rake your fingernails through my dirt,
paint my blood into the earth.
I wanted my brain to ricochet your name
off the soft tissue of my heart:
echoes of love still hanging on.

You touched me like a homecoming,
and my skin heralded your arrival.
I spoke more in sighs and whispers
than I ever did to you in words.
We were so busy making love,
that we never got the chance to fuck,
and I wanted you down into my bone marrow.

I wanted your lips to fuse with me,
I wanted you to leave me bruises
to count like stars in the morning.
I wanted to love you in the light of day,
but the moon always got the front-row seat.

If that wasn't tragedy enough,
with every new frame whose curves you trace
as your body count climbs higher,
I swear, I can feel it:
a feathered specter on my spine.

More than anything,
I *despise*
that I never stood
the test of time.

In my dreams,
you *conjure* me
like a spell in the night.

Let us haunt one another
with uneasy peace,

and die b u r n i n g alive.

You loved me *too softly,*
so damned softly,
that you never bothered
to salvage my bones
after loving my skin to oblivion.

I'd have built you a h o m e of them.

Oh, I was such a fool for you,
a beautiful little fool.

I was always *gone*,
a softly blinking "exit" sign.
I became a question mark,
a whispered suspicion,
a piece of trace evidence:
lights on, nobody home,
door always slightly open,
like the moment before you find the body.

They'd have found mine on **yours.**

You brought a screaming vibrancy
to every facet of my days.

In the aftermath,
I learned more than ever before
about the nuances of grey.

I memorized the sound
of the second hand,
ticking you further away from me.

Grey memories.
Grey walls.
Grey music.
Grey loss.
Grey ghosts of us
haunting these halls,
feigning harmlessness.

If all was to remain so colorless,
the least I could do
was stop every clock
at the moment that you left.

Only once everything
was muted and stagnant
did this house feel like home again.

I inhabit the quiet
that you left behind,
and you occupy
every corner of my mind.

Shades of Ruin

Sometimes,
I look toward *that* room,
now a tomb at
the end of my house.

Within its walls,
the remains of us
haunt our shut-door love
in the last place
where it roamed freely.

I dare not open the door,
for fear of what might slip out
and into me.

I didn't know how to *lay you to rest,*
so I've been doing it in   p i e c e s.

I've pulled little fragments of you
out of me by the roots,
at the expense of my own skin.

And that's just it...
real love   c-u-t-s you open.
To let you go is to lose a piece of myself.

Hell is a place on earth.
It is right here:
me living out my days without you.

I've got this shallow grave,
this not-so-final resting place
dug right   in the middle   of my life.

So I cling on to our memories,
and wish you were **still beside me.**

Shades of Ruin

Sometimes,
on Saturday nights,
I put the bottle to my head
and pull the trigger,
my hands shaking out your name
until I'm drunk enough to forget my own,
until I can hold nothing else

but the memory of our love.

Drinking to forget:
I never understood that.

All it does is melt away my defenses,
dismantle my armor,
round off the sharp edges of my stubbornness,
and strip me naked
down to the memory of you.

It leaves me desperate,
frantically typing messages
I always end up deleting,
rehearsing undelivered speeches
through the haze of a foggy head
that only clears the path to you.

I lose my grip on everything
every single time I drink
until all that's ever left is *you.*

Wait...
is that why I do it?

I don't recall what I was doing
when it suddenly dawned on me
that I no longer remembered your scent.
It seems the wind carried it away
from my memory,
and it must have left
in the same cardinal direction
that you first walked away from me.

Your North Star summoned you away,
and she isn't me, so I had no further claim.
The scent of fate trailed me tauntingly
as you left the center of my gravity.
It was then when I fell
from the night's tapestry,
an unlucky star destined to burn alone,
unwished upon.

I buried a broken wishbone
beneath a headstone that read:
"Here lies every bet I ever placed on you".

To tell you the soul-crushing truth,
some space within me was suddenly empty.
The scent of you used to stay with me for days.
You would seep into my clothing
the way you did my heart:
starting slowly and gently,
and then suddenly all at once.
You'd cling to my hair,
splayed on pillows after dark.

I remember...

Three months later,
as the well was finally beginning to dry,
crumpled at the back of my closet, I found it:
The Dress I wore
on what I didn't know would be our last night.

→

Shades of Ruin

I erased time back to midnight sighs,
to the warmth of shared skin,
and to the delicate rush of searching lips
between the throes of barely whispered prose.

I pressed The Dress to my nose,
and found what was left of your ghost.

I sank to the floor and cried.

I last saw you just over a year later,
in the dim glow of late August twilight;
the fire from the dwindling summer sky
had nothing on the light in our eyes.
In that moment (I never told you this),
inhaling you was the first thing I did.
Your arms welcomed me home
since your lips weren't allowed to anymore.
I wished for the core of that memory
never to fade.

It did.

It faded somewhere inside the borrowed time
between longing and regret.

I swore I wouldn't forget;
that was my first broken promise.

Someday,
I hope to catch your scent upon the breeze.
Was no part of you ever truly mine to keep?

How do thoughts of you
always manage to come rushing back
and *steal* what little peace I have?

Shades of Ruin

This silence is killing me,
so I rebel as loudly as I can,
holding off quiet death by inches.

I chase it away by creating
as much noise as I can manage,
sending every object you once touched
sailing to the ground,
crash-landing in our wreckage.

I sing at the top of defeated lungs
that once confused love of you with oxygen.
I get into bed and touch away your memory
until I am filling the air with screams.

Anything to *drown you out*;
this silence is *killing* me.

And I swear it that even now,
I hear the sound of your breathing
in the silence.

The quiet nearly drives me to insanity;
I can't drive you from my mind.

Wherever my thoughts go,
wherever my body roams,
you're never far behind.

So it goes,
you never needed to touch me
to hold me close.

I go down to the river,
and I drop you like a stone
deep
          beneath
                    the
                              water.

The trouble is,
I know exactly where I left you...

and I've always been a strong swimmer.

No matter how my life changes,
no matter where the journey takes me,
the time I spent with you
will always keep me warm.

In some small way,
you will always be mine,

and I will always be yours.

Shades of Ruin

Years later, we are still dying plants,
broken objects on their last leg,
stars falling for a fever dream
that we know we'll never have.

Your lungs run on oxygen,
your heart runs on false reasons,
my blood pumps through veins
that refuse to change with the seasons.

It is torture to see you out there
living a life I can't climb inside,
and you hate watching my stories,
but it's the only way you breathe.

I land into and through you
like shrapnel to your organs,
and you're all over me
like a sleepless night.

We both live to fantasize
about suddenly taking off,
two thieves in the dead of night,
getting off on getting lost.

We'd drive to a new life,
and love each other
as *loudly* as we want.

I can't unlove you,
you can't forget me.
I've tried to, you've cried to,
but we're deaf to the screams
of blessings and blasphemy.

The air holds your voice,
I hear you through the noise
in a million tiny echoes,
so I store it in my soul:
gravel road and autumn gold.

Let go
let go
let go
I won't

Every changing channel
in motion-capture mute,
you manage to come through.
I catch you in the static,
I hear you in the music.

Full moon and half life,
we bleed, lonely in the night,
both lost and neither found.
Play me all our saddest songs,
put me in the ground.

Wake up
wake up
wake up
I won't

Life on autopilot,
did I forget how to drive?
I guess we were no accident,
but we crash-landed,
twisted up by time.

→

Shades of Ruin

They took us in
on separate gurneys,
but didn't set the limbs.
We never healed right,
and now we both live broken.

Move on
move on
move on
I won't

I just cut the brake line
speeding down the highway,
songs and signs and neon lights
all point to yesterday.

I sing your name in grey,
because it's all I know.

Come home
come home
come home
you won't

It won't be long,
it won't be long now.
I'll try again someday,
I won't let go,
I don't know how.

And I'll sleep in the passenger seat,
the *ghost of you driving me home.*

You miss me in a way
that does not quite make sense,
but you never know where to put it:
I do not fit in your pockets,
or your heart, or your head.

Days bleed into weeks,
weeks bleed into months,
months bleed into years;
I look around,
and you're still not here.

When you run across my mind,
(which happens more often
than I'd like to admit),
I gather up all of the love I can,
and send it in your general direction.

I have learned to love you
in my own, silent way,
wishing you all the beauty life can bring
for the rest of your days,
even
      if
            they
                  won't
                        include
                              me.

All your life,
I know that a piece of you
will long for me.

I cracked you open long ago,
and the crevices created by my love
will *never* close.

It's the nearness that I miss,
the proximity to you
that could either slow or race
my heartbeat into wild embers.

My pulse would quicken.
My bones would settle.
My mind would find stillness.
My body would remember rest.

You could both light me on fire
and blanket me in ocean.

...what if I never find that again?

Shades of Ruin

It's a war to keep you here,
and I've spent *years* on the front lines.

I will not armor up any longer;
these trenches hold no glory.

I will lay my sword
and a white flag at your feet,
and walk off the hill
with a still-beating heart
that will one day race
for someone else...

even if I can't picture it now.

It was the way your hands
found me most easily in the dark,
the way we could taste the universe
when the other was close enough.

I will never forget
How *beautiful* we were.

Shades of Ruin

Our memories lurch
to a reluctant halt
in their funeral march
so my eyes can pour salt
over them *one last time.*

Once more, for goodbye.

Stefanie Briar

Hand in hand, we walk deserted streets,
kissing on the white lines in all my dreams.

The rain is soft silver on the pavement,
and I paint you into every portrait.

We walk slowly to the home we share,
and never make it past the stairs.

We set the place on fire,
bodies colliding like stars in our irises.

Our tangled limbs are infinite,
and I keep you close inside.

These are the lullabies
behind my eyes each night.
It's no wonder every sunrise
feels like a new goodbye.

The day breaks,
and I wish you'd stay, but oh,

how *beautifully* you fade...

Maybe, in the end,
there will be quiet between us.
Maybe there will be no symphony,
no giant sign heralding our love in neon.
Maybe there will be no wildfires,
no weeping audience, no closing credits.

Maybe there will be only souldust,
a coastline to ripple the pull of the moon.
Maybe the music, the blinking arrows,
the inferno, the tears, and the closure
will all be soft:
the atmosphere unchanged
by the gravity of us.

Maybe there will be a sacred knowing
that passes between us,
an exchange that speaks
beyond the curvatures of lips
that we sailed like anchors into one another.

Maybe we will float, suspended but never lost,
frozen in motion toward
the only truth we know.
Maybe we will not stir or move,
but will hold one another just the same.
Maybe you'll send the rain,
and I'll hang the sun,
and we'll go out on a rainbow.

Maybe we'll feel the entirety of a lifetime
vibrating off of the skin we borrowed,
becoming the symphony,
and the fire, and the flood,

and the film
where the end

is

n e v e r

ours.

I never needed us
to last a lifetime
to know that your name
will hang upon my lips
until the moment I take
my *final breath.*

Shades of Ruin

I have bled us,
our love, our lifeblood,
drop by crimson drop
onto umpteen pages of poetry,
granting you unintentional immortality.

I find it strangely comforting:
we had one lovely, final conversation,
that cruel, hopeful last rally,
the last good day
before the inevitable succumbing.

We went out like a whisper,
with memories on our lips,
lifetimes in our eyes
and love upon our tongues.

We were felled by the death knell
of two hearts that, once connected,
were never again able to beat separately.

Quietly, the pen falls from my hand,
never to write of us again.
May we rest in tender pieces.

I close the pages of our story,
press you into the bindings
of books I never meant to write,
releasing you like I was told to
so many times.

There are two candles left on my writing desk
that I accidentally left burning.
I extinguish them,
committing our last breath
to the ether of eternity.

Wisps of smoke send us off,
and I close my eyes
to the scent of roses and parchment.

I open them,
standing small upon clean pages
I cannot see the end of.

We were the ride of a lifetime.

Acknowledgements

My love, for supporting me through and through with unending faith.

My tribe, for walking alongside me no matter the journey.

My readers, for giving the pieces of my soul a home.

Mitch, for bringing this story to stunning life with your art. No one else could have done this cover.

Melissa, for being my earth angel and my first set of eyes.

Novo Amor, for providing the otherworldly music that I wrote so much of this book while listening to.

About the Author

Stefanie Briar is a poet, lyricist, educator, and freelance editor best known for her bestselling poetry collection, *Burn.*

She is a Potterhead and Swiftie who enjoys candles, cancelled plans, and witchy shit. She lives for great music and the power of telling a good story.

She shares her New Jersey home with her husband, daughter, cat, and python.

Connect with her:

@stefanie.briar.poetry

@stefaniebriarpoetry

Other titles by Stefanie Briar:

Cosmosis
Homecoming
Burn

Shades of Ruin:
The soundtrack

For a more immersive experience, scan the
following code into Spotify.

This varied and evocative playlist captures
the essence of the book.

Printed in Great Britain
by Amazon

24149215R00045